Test Yourself for
FIRST CERTIFICATE

Susan Morris

•

Alan Stanton

Nelson

Thomas Nelson and Sons Ltd
Nelson House   Mayfield Road
Walton-on-Thames Surrey
KT12 5PL UK

51 York Place
Edinburgh
EH1 3JD UK

Thomas Nelson (Hong Kong) Ltd
Toppan Building 10/F
22A Westlands Road
Quarry Bay   Hong Kong

© Susan Morris and Alan Stanton 1989

First published by Thomas Nelson and Sons Ltd 1989

ISBN 0–17–555737–3

NPN 9 8 7 6 5 4 3

Printed and bound in Hong Kong

Contents

Notes to the Student

The Cambridge First Certificate in English Examination consists of five papers:

Paper 1 – Reading Comprehension (1 hour)
Paper 2 – Composition (1½ hours)
Paper 3 – Use of English (2 hours)
Paper 4 – Listening Comprehension (20–30 minutes)
Paper 5 – Interview (about 12 minutes)

Test Yourself for First Certificate is especially designed for self-access use by students preparing for this examination. It contains ten 'mini tests' in exam format, giving intensive practice in Paper 1, Section A (Reading Comprehension) and Paper 3 (Use of English) excluding Directed Writing. The question types in these papers test your vocabulary and knowledge of grammar and structure. After each test you can quickly check your progress by using the Key at the back of the book, which provides answers and guidelines for marking.

How to use this book

Reading Comprehension, Section A
You should answer every one of these multiple choice questions. If you don't know the correct answer, try eliminating the wrong ones. If you really don't know the answer, it is better to guess than to leave the question unanswered.

Use of English
Question 1: Read the whole passage carefully at least twice before you begin to fill the gaps. Complete each gap with one word only. If you are stuck and aren't sure what to put:

- try telling the story to yourself
- look at the grammar of the sentences for clues
- remember that the missing words are often structural words, such as parts of the verb or prepositions. Check through the ones you know to see if you can find one to fit.

Question 2: This tests your knowledge of grammar. Try to identify the structure that is being tested (for example, passives, reported speech, conditional sentences, etc).

Questions 3 and 4: All the phrasal verbs tested are listed in the *Cambridge English Lexicon*. Remember that the verb must be put in the correct tense. The vocabulary questions are based on common, everyday topics (for example, houses, food, clothes). Check whether you need a singular or plural form.

Question 5: Every oblique (/) indicates one or more words missing. The words that you need to add are short, structural words (such as *which, that, some, from, since, the, etc.*). You must not change the order of the words given. Verbs are given in the infinitive form, so you must look for words which help you choose the right tense (for example, 'yesterday' indicates a past tense).

Lastly, it's a good idea to keep a total of your score when you check the answers, so that you can measure your progress as you work through the tests.

Test 1

Reading Comprehension, Section A

Choose the word or phrase (A, B, C, or D) which best completes each sentence.

1   The ....A........ from London to Bristol takes two hours by car.
    A journey   B travel   C driving   D voyage

2   Gerald went to the bank to ....A....... his drachmas into pounds.
    A exchange   B convert   C change   D turn

3   Steven couldn't understand the language ....C........ , but after a few weeks he
    could communicate quite well.
    A first of all   B first   C at first   D firstly

4   Charles Dickens ....D........ on 9 June 1870.
    A die   B death   C dead   D died

5   Soon after reaching the scene of the accident in Grosvenor Square the
    policeman took the names and addresses of ......A......... .
    A witnesses   B onlookers   C watchers   D spectators

6   Sarah wanted to buy some shoes to ....A........ her new dress.
    A match   B suit   C fit   D resemble

7   If the firemen ....D....... the correct address, they would have got to the fire
    more quickly.
    A would have   B were having   C have had   D had had

8   Michael read two novels ....B........ the flight to Singapore.
    A for   B during   C while   D through

9   We are all looking forward ....C........ you when you next come to England.
    A see   B to see   C to seeing   D for seeing

10 We have been ....A........ business with that company since 1960.
    A doing   B making   C growing   D working

11 The caller asked to be put ....A........ to the manager.
    A through   B over   C on   D off

12 At the age of eighteen he .... the army.
A enlisted   B conscripted   C entered   D joined

13 The station clock isn't ....
A timely   B precise   C right   D correct

14 He left the lights on to make it look .... the house was occupied.
A so that   B as for   C so far   D as if

15 The storm did considerable .... to the trees in the park.
A harm   B damage   C destruction   D injury

16 The delay at the airport .... that we arrived at our hotel three hours later than planned.
A resulted   B led   C meant   D caused

17 He was offered the job of managing director but he turned it ....
A off   B over   C up   D down

18 Sally was .... of her purse by two young men.
A robbed   B taken   C stolen   D grabbed

19 Climbing boots and helmets were provided so we .... bring our own.
A didn't need to   B needn't have   C not needed   D need not

20 What does that notice .... ?
A print   B write   C say   D tell

21 Can you look .... the children for an hour while I go shopping?
A after   B out   C for   D to

22 In this hot weather milk will turn .... very quickly unless you put it in the fridge immediately.
A bitter   B bad   C thick   D sour

23 They gave me .... advice about what to say in the interview.
A an   B plenty of   C some of   D the

24 I need £1,000 to pay off the debt, but I just haven't got ....
A them   B some   C these   D it

25 The manager told us that a great .... of money was missing.
A lot   B quantity   C deal   D supply

Use of English

1 *Fill each of the numbered blanks in the following passage. Use only* **one** *word in each space.*

One Saturday, Henry Dombey was in his jewellery shop, waiting for customers. At 10 a.m., ... (1) first customer, a smartly-dressed, middle-aged man arrived and, after looking around, ... (2) a £400 watch, which he paid for .... (3) cheque.

Half an hour later, the same customer returned to the shop with .... (4) waiter from a .... (5) cafe. He was trying to sell the watch to the waiter for £200 cash .... (6) wanted Mr Dombey to confirm that the watch was worth at .... (7) that much. Mr Dombey became very suspicious and called the police. He assumed that the cheque was .... (8), since otherwise the customer would have lost £200. When the police arrived, the customer explained that, after .... (9) the shop, he had .... (10) remembered an important business meeting in Manchester .... (11) afternoon. He realised that he didn't have enough cash to cover his expenses, so he had .... (12) to sell the watch because the meeting was more important .... (13) losing £200. Mr Dombey didn't believe this and neither .... (14) the police, and the customer .... (15) arrested.

Mr Dombey was very surprised when, on Monday, the bank paid the cheque without question. He was .... (16) more surprised when, on Tuesday, he received a letter from the customer's lawyers telling .... (17) he was .... (18) to be taken to court .... (19) making false accusations. Eventually, Mr Dombey had to pay £5,000 in compensation to the customer.

It was, of course, an elaborate trick .... (20) the customer had planned very carefully.

2 *Finish each of the following sentences in such a way that it means exactly the same as the sentence printed before it.*

      EXAMPLE: I haven't enjoyed myself so much for ages.

      ANSWER: It's ages *since I enjoyed myself so much.*

a) It's five years since I last visited Peru.

   I haven't ....

b) It would be a good idea to buy a dictionary if you want to learn a foreign language.

   You'd better ....

c) Whose pen is this?

   Who ....

d) Rosalind is so hardworking that she is sure to get on in her job.

   Rosalind is such ....

e) Electrical activity in the brain is recorded by this machine.

   This machine ....

f) Eat up your vegetables or you won't get any pudding.

   If you ....

g) Although Alfred was over seventy, he continued to cycle to work every day.

   Despite ....

h) 'Sebastian is the one who stole the video-recorder,' said Bernard.

   Bernard accused ....

i) This is the best apple-pie I have ever tasted.

   I have ....

j) Please don't invite Mary to stay for the weekend.

   I'd rather ....

3 *Complete the following sentences with a phrase made from* **bring**. *Write one word in each blank space.*

EXAMPLE: A series of financial scandals *brought down* the government.

a) The Prime Minister aimed to .... a change in people's attitude to private enterprise.

b) 'When I got home, I discovered that the video tape I had bought was faulty, so I've .... it .... to change it,' I said to the shop assistant.

c) I wanted to know if Denys had really left his wife, but I didn't like to .... the subject .... in front of the children.

d) I know it's difficult if you want to do something and your father won't let you. Can't your mother help to .... him .... ?

e) Anna wanted to show Margaret the photos of her holiday so she .... her photo album.

4 *Complete each of the following sentences with one word which refers to* **using the telephone**.

EXAMPLE: If you give me your *number*, I'll ring you tonight.

a) I rang the office and asked the .... to put me through to Stephen.

b) When you ring the office, you'll get through faster if you ask for my .... , which is 792, instead of asking for me by name.

c) I've tried the number four times already, but it's always ....

d) If you don't know someone's number, try looking it up in the telephone ....

e) Pick up the receiver and then .... the number.

5 *Make all the changes and additions necessary to produce, from the following sets of words and phrases, sentences which together make a complete letter. Note carefully from the example what kind of alterations need to be made. Write each sentence in the space provided.*

      EXAMPLE: I be very surprised/receive/letter/you yesterday.

      ANSWER: *I was very surprised to receive a letter from you yesterday.*

17 avenue des lilas
Toulon
France

17 June 19– –

The Principal
Brighton English Study Centre
Brighton BN1 7TP

Dear Sir,

A friend/mine/attend/school/1986/1987/recommend/it/to me.

a) ....

I want/spend/year/England/improve/English before go/university.

b) ....

I/already study English/six years/school.

c) ....

I/like/attend/course/general English/first two terms/then study Business English.

d) ....

I be interested/take exams/I/be/school.

e) ....

Could you tell me/exams I enrol/I/have/pay/enter/them?

f) ....

Finally/you send me/prospectus/full details/how much everything cost?

g) ....

I hope/hear/you soon.

h) ....

Yours faithfully,

Serena Blanc

Test 2

Reading Comprehension, Section A

Choose the word or phrase (A, B, C, or D) which best completes each sentence.

1 Tom's mother doesn't .... of eating between meals.
   A approve   B agree   C accept   D allow

2 The .... of the football team led his side to victory in a close match.
   A manager   B coach   C trainer   D captain

3 I had difficulty driving the car because I wasn't .... with the controls.
   A accustomed   B familiar   C acquainted   D used

4 Clarissa took a great .... of trouble over the dinner party for her boss.
   A number   B deal   C body   D lot

5 Robert Smith .... to take over as manager of the company.
   A accepted   B complied   C submitted   D agreed

6 The test flight had to be postponed on .... of the bad weather.
   A owing   B account   C reason   D cause

7 The information given in the report is not ....
   A truthful   B precise   C accurate   D concise

8 I've got a(n) .... in my back.
   A pain   B ache   C soreness   D hurt

9 The Director of Public Prosecutions decided there was not sufficient evidence
   to allow him to .... action against the man suspected of gold smuggling.
   A allow   B take   C make   D pursue

10 Vesuvius is no longer a(n) .... volcano.
    A erupting   B live   C lively   D active

11 If you get a poor picture on the TV, try .... the aerial.
    A manipulating   B waving   C adjusting   D positioning

12 Philip .... he had cheated during the competition.
A admitted   B agreed   C exclaimed   D swore

13 The Department of Transport gave .... warning that a section of the motorway would be closed for two days.
A prior   B beforehand   C advance   D previous

14 Alan Sampson acted as a double ...., spying for one country while pretending to spy for another.
A agent   B spy   C traitor   D defector

15 The soldier .... his rifle at the civilian.
A directed   B aimed   C targetted   D positioned

16 The burglar forced a window and .... the alarm.
A set off   B stimulated   C raised   D turned on

17 My brother is .... to succeed in his profession.
A ambitious   B serious   C committed   D keen

18 I don't believe that Robert is capable .... such cruelty.
A for   B to   C by   D of

19 Neil's boss was very annoyed .... him when he asked for a week's holiday during the busiest time of the year.
A with   B by   C at   D for

20 Sally tried to get the cotton .... the eye of the needle.
A to   B through   C in   D out

21 Do you think the new girl has settled down .... the job?
A with   B at   C in   D by

22 Jeffrey got his first job .... answering an advertisement in the newspaper.
A for   B out of   C from   D by

23 .... your father gets a new job away from home, will you go with him?
A Supposing   B Providing   C Saying   D Pretending

24 You'd .... hurry up or else you'll be late.
A have to   B better   C rather   D prefer

25 If anyone .... had been so rude to the Prime Minister, he'd have lost his temper.
A besides   B other   C else   D whoever

Use of English

1 *Fill each of the numbered blanks in the following passage. Use only* **one** *word in each space.*

Renata Smith, a divorced mother of two young girls, Sabrina aged ten and Joey aged six, lives in Sheffield. She is typical of today's one-parent single-income families .... (1) on the breadline struggling to make ends meet.

Renata .... (2) working as a secretary in the city when she met Tom, a lorry driver, at a party. They went out .... (3) for six months and then they decided to .... (4) married. At first she and Tom lived with her parents but then, when Renata was .... (5) Sabrina, they moved into .... (6) council flat. Tom had to spend a lot of time .... (7) from home and, soon after the .... (8) of their second child, he left Renata to live in another city.

Renata set about .... (9) up the girls on .... (10) own, though her mother was always .... (11) to help when she could. Money was the most pressing problem, and Renata, ... (12) had given up her job when Sabrina was born, had to look for work. After two months she .... (13) to find a post as Personal Assistant to the Sales Director of a local company. She .... (14) been working there .... (15) nearly two years now and enjoys spending her days in the office. When she's not .... (16) work, the girls have priority. .... (17) are the most important thing in her life, and she is determined to be .... (18) mother and father to them. She doesn't want them to suffer from the .... (19) that their father does not live with them, and she does everything possible to provide them .... (20) a rich and rewarding life.

2 *Finish each of the following sentences in such a way that it means exactly the same as the sentence printed before it.*

   EXAMPLE: I haven't enjoyed myself so much for ages.

   ANSWER: It's ages *since I enjoyed myself so much.*

a) The winter in England is too cold for gardeners to leave geraniums outside.

   The winter in England is not _____

b) Peter's grandfather came to live in England fifty years ago.

   Peter's grandfather has _____

c) The fireman managed to rescue the child from the burning house.

   The fireman was _____

d) Stephen would rather windsurf than sail.

   Stephen prefers_____

e) Mary will only come to the party if Peter is invited.

   Unless Peter_____

f) We really must leave the party now if we are to catch the last bus.

   It's time we _____

g) 'I'm sorry I lost your book, Geraldine,' said Michael.

   Michael apologised_____

h) The patient's temperature must be checked every hour.

   You have _____

i) That suit is too expensive for me.

   I haven't got _____

j) Despite not speaking a word of French, Jeremy decided to make his home in Paris.

   Although _____

3   *Complete the following sentences with a phrase made from* **get**. *Write one word in each blank space.*

   EXAMPLE: He always *gets up* at 7 a.m.

   a)   I've tried to explain already, but I just don't know how to .... it
        .... to him.

   b)   Michael left the flat because he just couldn't ....
        .... his flatmates.

   c)   Would anyone like to suggest a way of .... this
        problem?

   d)   'The bullet is in a very difficult position. I'm not sure how we can
        .... it,' said the surgeon.

   e)   Bill Sikes thought he had .... his crimes
        until he opened his front door and saw four policemen standing there.

4   *The word in capitals at the end of each of the following sentences can be used to form a word that fits suitably in the blank space. Fill each blank in this way.*

   EXAMPLE: He was *famous* as a singer of romantic songs.   FAME

   a)   The snow and ice made the steps very ....   SLIP

   b)   Do you know the .... of this word?   PRONOUNCE

   c)   The .... of the club has now reached 1,000.   MEMBER

   d)   There is no .... on this cheque.   SIGN

   e)   The United Kingdom exports a large number of different ....
                                                                  PRODUCE

5   *Make all the changes and additions necessary to produce, from the following sets of words and phrases, sentences which together make a complete letter. Note carefully from the example what kind of alterations need to be made. Write each sentence in the space provided.*

   EXAMPLE: I be very surprised/receive/letter/you yesterday.

   ANSWER: *I was very surprised to receive a letter from you yesterday.*

26 Cathedral Road
Cardiff
CF5 2DD

24 May 19– –

Dear Maria,

It be lovely/hear/you/Monday.

a) ....

Martin/I be delighted/learn/forthcoming wedding.

b) ....

Of course we absolutely love/be there/big day/unfortunately it/just impossible.

c) ....

In July Martin attend a conference/San Francisco/California/new developments/
electronics.

d) ....

He arrange/me/go/him/almost all/arrangements now be made.

e) ....

We stay/ States/conference/go/tour/five more states.

f) ....

I be very sorry/this mean we not be/your wedding/you know/you have/very best
wishes.

g) ....

We already post/present/we hope you/Karl like it.

h) ....

With very best wishes,
Catherine

Test 3

Reading Comprehension, Section A

Choose the word or phrase (A, B, C, or D) which best completes each sentence.

1   Martin switched on the radio to catch the latest ....
    A news   B notices   C broadcasts   D programmes

2   We went to a(n) .... of paintings by Goya.
    A display   B show   C exhibition   D exposition

3   I thought I was late but then I realised my watch was ten minutes ....
    A early   B fast   C ahead   D in advance

4   I'm sorry I'm late – I was held .... by the traffic.
    A in   B up   C back   D over

5   Any claim for .... must be received within seven days.
    A breakages   B breaks   C break-ups   D breaking

6   The .... of pay is £22.50 per hour.
    A rate   B level   C limit   D wage

7   When he stood outside the theatre he could hear the sound of .... inside.
    A laugh   B laughter   C laughs   D laughed

8   There is no .... for this disease.
    A help   B remedy   C cure   D aid

9   We expected to find a .... in the village who would take us through the mountains.
    A leader   B mountaineer   C director   D guide

10 Charles Dickens .... on 7 February 1812.
    A born   B birth   C is born   D was born

11 Adrian decided to go to the fancy .... party as a Roman senator.
    A costume   B clothes   C dress   D habit

12 Sylvester wasn't sure if the medicine would make his hair grow again but he decided to give it a(n) ....
A turn   B effort   C experiment   D try

13 The minister was .... speak when a shot rang out.
A on the point of   B just   C nearly   D about to

14 Brian moved into the outside .... to overtake a lorry.
A lane   B channel   C road   D route

15 Take these sandwiches .... you feel hungry while watching the match.
A that   B so far   C in case   D although

16 Be careful you don't .... your keys!
A loose   B lose   C to lose   D loosen

17 The council decided to .... the road to improve the traffic flow.
A broaden   B increase   C widen   D enlarge

18 Susan knew many of Browning's poems .... heart.
A with   B to   C from   D by

19 I'm afraid Richard hasn't got .... his illness yet.
A through   B up   C over   D out

20 Thank you for .... me about the meeting this afternoon.
A reminding   B remember   C remembering   D remind

21 Paolo's restaurant has been .... recommended in the guide-books.
A mainly   B extremely   C highly   D mostly

22 .... person who damages the trees in the park will be prosecuted.
A Some   B All   C The   D Any

23 The lorry-driver admitted he was .... for the accident.
A blame   B fault   C responsible   D cause

24 Sarah decided to do an additional .... in computer programming.
A career   B election   C subject   D course

25 'I'm afraid we don't have that model in ....,' said the shopkeeper.
A supply   B stock   C storage   D order

Use of English

1 *Fill each of the numbered blanks in the following passage. Use only **one** word in each space.*

In 1914, Ernest Shackleton, the famous polar explorer, headed towards Antarctica in the *Endurance*. He and his twenty-eight companions intended to cross Antarctica .... (1) foot.

However, their ship became stuck in the ice, and, ... (2) it had been built for these conditions, ... (3) slowly crushed by the pressure of the ice. It was not possible .... (4) Shackleton and his men to travel over the frozen sea to the .... (5) land, four hundred kilometres away, because the ice was not flat and smooth. It was raised up into high ridges .... (6) were often impassable. Moreover, the ice was .... (7) up into large pieces which moved .... (8) to the wind and current.

.... (9) their six months on the ice, Shackleton's men survived .... (10) eating their dogs, and penguins and seals .... (11) they could catch them. Eventually, they .... (12) Elephant Island, which was uninhabited. In a small boat .... (13) had taken from the ship, Shackleton and six of his men sailed for over eight hundred miles to .... (14) island where they knew .... (15) was a whaling-station, and therefore food, shelter and a radio. Their boat landed on the wrong side of the island .... (16) they had to climb a mountain range and march sixty kilometres .... (17) safety. Shackleton then arranged .... (18) a ship to collect his twenty-two companions on Elephant Island.

It is because .... (19) his superb powers of organisation and leadership that .... (20) his men survived this terrible experience.

2 *Finish each of the following sentences in such a way that it means exactly the same as the sentence printed before it.*

EXAMPLE: I haven't enjoyed myself so much for ages.

ANSWER: It's ages *since I enjoyed myself so much.*

a) Who does this bicycle belong to?

Whose ....

b) Do you feel like going for a walk in the park?

Would you like ....

c) It's more than ten years since I last saw a play by Christopher Marlowe.

I haven't ....

d) The weather was so cold that people only went out if they had to.

It was ....

e) Alison apologised for being late.

'I'm ....

f) Although Frederick had only one arm, he became famous as a mountaineer.

In spite ....

g) Margaret has read more books than any one else in the class.

No-one ....

h) Henry's got toothache because he doesn't go to the dentist for regular check-ups.

If Henry ....

i) These shoes still need mending.

These shoes haven't ....

j) It's a pity I haven't got a new dress to wear to the party.

I wish ....

3 *Complete the following sentences with a phrase made from* **make**. *Write one word in each blank space.*

    EXAMPLE: It took the actor three hours to *make up* his face.

a) The desert patrol decided to .... the nearest oasis.

b) It was too dark for the policeman to .... the number of the speeding car.

c) In court, the witness admitted that he had .... the story ....

d) The large bonus payment Mr Price received didn't really .... the loss of his job.

e) 'Shall I .... the bill now, madam?'

4 *The word in capitals at the end of each of the following sentences can be used to form a word that fits suitably in the blank space. Fill each blank in this way.*

    EXAMPLE: He was *famous* as a singer of romantic songs.   FAME

a) You had better take this radio back to the shop because it is ....   FAULT

b) The athlete aimed for a peak of physical ....   FIT

c) The .... men put all the furniture into the van.   REMOVE

d) What is the .... of this container?   WEIGH

e) This is the most .... order we have ever received.   VALUE

5 *In the travel agent's, a customer is trying to get information about how to travel from London to Paris. Complete the dialogue.*

CUSTOMER	Hello. I want to travel from London to Paris on 28 June. (1) How ....?
TRAVEL AGENT	Well, there are quite a few different ways. There's flying, of course.
CUSTOMER	(2) Isn't ....?
TRAVEL AGENT	Yes, there are certainly a lot of cheaper ways. There's the train, well it's train, ferry, train in fact.
CUSTOMER	(3) How ....?
TRAVEL AGENT	It's £39 single and £59.50 return.
CUSTOMER	(4) How ....?
TRAVEL AGENT	There are a number of trains throughout the day from early morning to late at night, so you can more or less choose the time that suits you best.
CUSTOMER	(5) How long ....?
TRAVEL AGENT	From London Victoria to Paris Gare de Lyon it's about seven hours.
CUSTOMER	(6) Are ....?
TRAVEL AGENT	No, there's the hovercraft, and you can also go by coach.
CUSTOMER	(7) So which is ....?
TRAVEL AGENT	The coach, although it takes a couple of hours longer than the train. It costs just £22.50 single.
CUSTOMER	Could you give me all the details about that, please? It'll suit my budget best.

Test 4

Reading Comprehension, Section A

Choose the word or phrase (A, B, C or D) which best completes each sentence.

1 Who are you going to vote .... in the election?
   A for   B with   C in   D to

2 Joan's very depressed .... the future.
   A with   B at   C about   D by

3 James and his wife now live ....
   A divided   B apart   C divorced   D separately

4 Helen and Tom had a blazing ....
   A quarrel   B argument   C disagreement   D row

5 I think Pepsi is inferior .... Coke.
   A than   B from   C to   D after

6 Alfred was rewarded .... his efforts in raising money for the people who
   suffered in the flood.
   A for   B by   C with   D out of

7 They fell in love at first ....
   A glance   B look   C sight   D view

8 Helen is suffering from a(n) .... of influenza.
   A outbreak   B attack   C infection   D symptom

9 The restaurant has been well decorated but somehow it lacks ....
   A atmosphere   B feeling   C sentiment   D warmth

10 My next door neighbours were absolutely thrilled .... the news of their
   son's success at the Olympics.
   A at   B through   C with   D from

11 Passengers should .... their seatbelts before the plane takes off.
   A secure   B tighten   C attach   D fasten

12 If you don't .... attention you won't understand what to do.
   A pay   B give   C get   D attract

13 If you want to get on in the company you'll have to change your .... to your work.
A relationship   B attitude   C opinion   D view

14 The .... watching the tennis match on TV couldn't really judge the accuracy of the shots.
A viewers   B audience   C spectators   D watchers

15 .... to an unexpected pay rise, we were able to repay the debt sooner than expected.
A Given   B In view   C Provided   D Thanks

16 I haven't quite finished the book yet, but I've got .... page 460.
A until   B as far   C up to   D through

17 We thoroughly enjoyed ourselves at the party .... there weren't many people there.
A however   B even   C although   D in spite

18 The judges of the competition decided not to .... the first prize because the standard was not high enough.
A award   B have   C give   D present

19 What is the applicant's family ....?
A origin   B background   C upbringing   D relationship

20 All the apples have .... bad.
A gone   B become   C turned   D got

21 The conference members all had to wear a .... to show who they were.
A name   B label   C tag   D badge

22 There are many ways to cook fish: one of the best is to .... it slowly in a dish in the oven.
A bake   B fry   C grill   D boil

23 Fred lost all his hair after the special medical treatment he had to have. He is now quite ....
A hairless   B naked   C bald   D shaved

24 All gymnasts have a highly developed sense of ....
A balance   B equilibrium   C steadiness   D gravity

25 Mike likes nothing better on a hot afternoon than sitting on the .... of the river.
A shore   B side   C edge   D bank

Use of English

1   *Fill each of the numbered blanks in the following passage. Use only* **one** *word in each space.*

At 6 p.m. on a cold, dark November day, Emma Woodhouse was driving home. She lived in a village .... (1) a remote part of the countryside and really depended .... (2) her car .... (3) the local bus service was so poor.

   At a crossroads, she saw an old lady .... (4) a shopping bag standing at a bus stop. As the car approached, the old lady raised .... (5) arm and Emma, thinking that she had missed the last bus, stopped and .... (6) her a lift. As they drove on, Emma .... (7) the old lady where she lived but .... (8) her surprise .... (9) was no answer. In fact, the old lady remained completely silent. Emma began to feel uneasy, especially .... (10) she noticed that the old lady had very large, hairy hands. .... (11), she had an idea. She stopped and said, 'I think one of the rear lights isn't working. Could you .... (12) out and check?' When the old lady was out of the car, Emma drove off. However, she began to feel guilty, thinking that she .... (13) abandoned a poor, old lady on .... (14) cold, wintry night; but she .... (15) not to go back.

   When she arrived .... (16), she noticed for the .... (17) time that the old lady's bag was .... (18) in the car. She was surprised, when she picked it up, to find that it was quite heavy, but imagine how she .... (19) when she opened it .... (20) saw that there was only one thing inside – an axe!

2   *Finish each of the following sentences in such a way that it means exactly the same as the sentence printed before it.*

    EXAMPLE: I haven't enjoyed myself so much for ages.

    ANSWER: It's ages *since I enjoyed myself so much.*

a)   How long have you been reading *Don Quixote*?

    When ....

b)   Peter managed to get promoted to the job of Office Manager because he worked extremely hard.

    By ....

c)   When we crossed the Alps, we couldn't see Mont Blanc because of the rain.

    If it ....

d)   I'm not tall enough to reach the shelf.

    The shelf is too high ....

e)   We have run out of milk.

    There ....

f)   That's the house where Charles Dickens lived from 1840 to 1850.

    That's the house Charles Dickens lived ....

g)   I'm sure it was Tom who cleared everything up.

    Tom must ....

h)   An enormous wave broke the ship in two.

    The ship ....

i)   Christabel doesn't have so far to travel as the other students.

    The other students ....

j)   Despite his lack of experience, I think he is the best man for the job.

    Although ....

3   *Complete the following sentences with a phrase made from* **turn***. Write one word in each blank space.*

EXAMPLE: Marianne *turned off* the light.

a)   Alice lost her chance of getting the job when she .... twenty minutes late for the interview.

b)   Bad weather forced the climbers to .... just before they reached the summit.

c)   Fairy stories are full of frogs .... princes and poor working girls becoming princesses.

d)   Frank was .... for the job because he didn't have sufficient experience.

e)   Although it was cloudy and cold in the morning, the afternoon .... fine.

4   *Complete each of the following sentences with one word which refers to* **something that is written***.*

EXAMPLE: He wrote a *report* on the problem and sent it to the manager.

a)   If you wish to be considered for this position, please complete the enclosed .... form and return it within fourteen days.

b)   We can supply sticky .... with your name and address at a cost of £2.50 per hundred.

c)   The teacher called out all the names on the ....

d)   The police wrote down what he told them and then asked him to sign the ....

e)   According to the .... we have to wear formal dress for this dinner.

5 *Make all the changes and additions necessary to produce, from the following sets of words and phrases, sentences which together make a complete letter. Note carefully from the example what kind of alterations need to be made. Write each sentence in the space provided.*

EXAMPLE: I be very surprised/receive/letter/you yesterday.

ANSWER: *I was very surprised to receive a letter from you yesterday.*

> 25 Adelaide Road
> Oxford
> OX1 2EK
>
> 7 July 19– –

Dear May

Well, Stephen/I/finally move/new flat/Oxford/we really love it.

a) ....

The flat/quite near/centre/we/not seem/get/noise.

b) ....

We/got/sitting-room, two bedrooms,/kitchen/ bathroom, in fact everything/ need/perfect home.

c) ....

We/like you/come/see us/soon/you possibly can.

d) ....

As you/see we/even got/spare room/you/stay in.

e) ....

We wonder/next weekend/be convenient/you/suit us perfectly.

f) ....

We be/home/evening/week.

g) ....

So just give/ring/if it be.

h) ....

Love

Anna

Test 5

Reading Comprehension, Section A

Choose the word or phrase (A, B, C or D) which best completes each sentence.

1 We arrived .... the airport two hours before our flight was due to leave.
  A in   B on   C at   D by

2 The fire was .... by a dropped match.
  A caused   B originated   C set off   D put in

3 His .... connections helped him to get a job with the company.
  A family   B familiar   C filial   D relative

4 There will be a .... of one hour before the departure of the train.
  A waiting   B lateness   C pause   D delay

5 At the newsagent's, John asked for the .... edition of *Golf Monthly*.
  A last   B latest   C actual   D present

6 When you come to see us next week, can you .... the children with you?
  A bring   B take   C fetch   D join

7 I haven't been able to finish the novel ....
  A still   B already   C yet   D now

8 Maria mistook the customer .... a shop assistant.
  A as   B being   C was   D for

9 After running for twenty kilometres, Adrian started to feel sharp .... in his knees.
  A pains   B aches   C hurts   D injuries

10 You .... better lock all the windows before we leave.
  A should   B must   C would   D had

11 If I .... you, I would accept their offer of a job.
  A be   B were   C would be   D was to be

12 When you make the sandwiches you will need twelve .... of bread per person.
    A loaves   B slices   C layers   D rolls

13 The police arrested him and .... him with murder.
    A accused   B blamed   C charged   D imprisoned

14 Bob is slowly getting used .... the new machines.
    A to operate   B operating   C to operating   D for operate

15 Professor Jones explained how to measure the .... of a mountain.
    A high   B highness   C rise   D height

16 Jack asked his bank manager for a £10,000 .... to buy a car.
    A loan   B discount   C charge   D request

17 The divers were warned to .... of sharks.
    A aware   B beware   C cautious   D guard

18 Nobody lives on that island because there is no source of .... water.
    A sweet   B good   C fresh   D drink

19 After three hours' work the painters took a ....
    A break   B pause   C turn   D wait

20 There is a standard £40 .... for a consultation with Dr Gilbertson.
    A rate   B cost   C expense   D fee

21 The magician invited members of the .... to come onto the stage.
    A crowd   B watchers   C fans   D audience

22 The ambulance men administered first .... to the injured.
    A help   B aid   C assistance   D treatment

23 Rupert selected the .... from which his suit would be made.
    A clothes   B cloth   C clothing   D cloths

24 James was desperate to get tickets for the tennis ....
    A contest   B court   C set   D match

25 I have no idea .... bag this is.
    A who   B who the   C who's   D whose

Use of English

1 *Fill each of the numbered blanks in the following passage. Use only* **one** *word in each space.*

Many English people feel a great deal of admiration for Queen Elizabeth I who .... (1) England from 1558 to 1603. Their admiration is based .... (2) the view of this queen as a strong and powerful woman, ... (3) possessed great political skills. .... (4), Elizabeth did not seem to have much happiness in her private life.

She was born in 1533, ... (5) daughter of the king, Henry VIII, and his second .... (6), Anne Boleyn. Henry had already divorced his first wife, Catherine of Aragon, ... (7) marry Elizabeth's mother, and in fact executed Anne Boleyn when their daughter was three. Elizabeth was a clever child, and was well taught, ... (8) her early years were not happy. When Henry died in 1547, Elizabeth's brother, Edward, became king at the age of nine. When he died, seven years .... (9), their elder sister Mary, a Roman Catholic, became queen. Elizabeth, herself a Protestant, suffered greatly .... (10) these years and was kept .... (11) a prisoner in the Tower of London.

Elizabeth finally became queen in 1558, when Mary died, and reigned over the country .... (12) 1603. During this period, English sailors established trade routes .... (13) over the world, and sometimes stole gold and silver .... (14) the ships of other nations. This activity, and also religious differences, ... (15) to conflict with Spain, the strongest and richest country .... (16) Europe in the sixteenth century. In 1588 Elizabeth's navy defeated an attempt .... (17) the Spanish to invade England.

Elizabeth had some proposals of marriage, but she never married. There was no shortage of men wishing to link .... (18) to her for political and other motives. But politics was her life and when she died, she left .... (19) united country much more powerful .... (20) the one over which she had inherited control.

2   *Finish each of the following sentences in such a way that it means exactly the same as the sentences printed before it.*

EXAMPLE: I haven't enjoyed myself so much for ages.

ANSWER: It's ages *since I enjoyed myself so much.*

a)   The bag was so light that Mary's three year-old son could carry it.

The bag was light ....

b)   Although he had been injured in the crash, he managed to walk twenty kilometres to get help.

In spite ....

c)   The boss's advice was so good that Robert would be foolish to ignore it.

Robert's boss gave ....

d)   Barbara will be twenty-five on October 23.

October 23 is ....

e)   'Why do I have to fill in so many forms?' asked Thomas.

Thomas asked...

f)   I didn't get as much information as I wanted.

I got ....

g)   Squadron-Leader Bigglesworth flew the aeroplane for the first time.

The aeroplane ....

h)   Could you open the window?

I wonder if you'd mind ....

i)   If I don't hear from you, I'll assume you can't come to the meeting.

Unless...

j)   My grandfather stopped driving five years ago.

My grandfather has ....

3 *Complete the following sentences with a phrase made from* **fall**. *Write one word in each blank space.*

    EXAMPLE: Because of illness, Martin has *fallen behind* with his work.

a) Sharon and Tracy used to be good friends but now they've ....
....

b) Captain Kirk's plans to organise an expedition to Antarctica have
...., but he hopes to try again next year.

c) James led at first but half-way through the race he began to ....
....

d) The first time Rita saw her future husband she immediately ....
.... him.

e) At university, Andrew .... a bad crowd.

4 *The word in capitals at the end of each of the following sentences can be used to form a word that fits suitably in the blank space. Fill each blank in this way.*

    EXAMPLE: He was *famous* as a singer of romantic songs.   FAME

a) His .... in the Olympic Games astonished everyone.   SUCCEED

b) This is a maximum .... area.   SECURE

c) You will need to get more .... before applying for such a job.

    QUALIFY

d) He was very .... of the films he had made.   PRIDE

e) Arnold lifted weights in order to increase his ....   STRONG

5 *Make all the changes and additions necessary to produce, from the following sets of words and phrases, sentences which together make a complete letter. Note carefully from the example what kind of alterations need to be made. Write each sentence in the space provided.*

    EXAMPLE: I be very surprised/receive/letter/you yesterday.

    ANSWER: *I was very surprised to receive a letter from you yesterday.*

71 Garden Road
Gloucester
GL6 7RE

6 August 19– –

Happy Tour Operators
Eastgate Street
Birmingham B3 2AA

Dear Sirs

I write/ you/say/dissatisfied I be/holiday/I just return.

a) ....

The holiday/Marbella be book/company/January.

b) ....

I understand/husband,/two children/I fly/Manchester/twelve noon/spend fourteen days/Hotel Esplendido/Marbella.

c) ....

We choose Hotel Esplendido/it have/private swimming pool, be/beach/offer/baby-sitting service/children.

d) ....

Our/flight/Manchester be delay/twenty-four hours/we have/spend/time/Departure Lounge.

e) ....

When we finally get/Marbella/representative tell us we be move/Hotel Blanco/be a forty-five minute walk/the beach.

f) ....

We not be satisfied/way we be treat/want/know/action you intend/take.

g) ....

We expect/refund/at least part/cost/trip.

h) ....

We look forward/hear/response.

i) ....

Yours faithfully

Ruth Brown (Mrs)

Test 6

Reading Comprehension, Section A

Choose the word or phrase (A, B, C, or D) which best completes each sentence.

1 In a market it's a good idea to .... to get a good price.
   A bargain   B argue   C dispute   D disagree

2 The dog .... when it saw the postman.
   A roared   B snapped   C barked   D gnarled

3 The bird broke the snail's shell by pecking at it with his ....
   A bill   B nose   C mouth   D beak

4 Couldn't you .... at the shops on your way home and get some food for supper?
   A call in   B pass by   C step in   D drop into

5 Bob and Alice have .... their wedding and decided to go their separate ways.
   A put off   B broken off   C called off   D written off

6 Sally .... doing gym by saying she had a headache.
   A got away with   B got out of   C got down to   D got into

7 If you're coming to stay in London, we'll be happy to .... you up.
   A put   B take   C turn   D get

8 Mary's son, James, missed three weeks of school because he was ill and then had lots to ....
   A find out   B get down to   C pick up   D catch up with

9 Tony had to wear a .... with his trousers because they were too loose.
   A strap   B tie   C lace   D belt

10 The car skidded on a slippery ....
   A bend   B turn   C turning   D corner

11 .... Anthony, who is coming to the party?
   A Also   B Besides   C Beside   D Apart

12 The ring wasn't .... what Elisabeth paid for it.
   A worth   B valuable   C value   D cost

13 Beverly was very .... for all the support his friends gave him when he lost
   his job.
   A obliged   B grateful   C pleased   D delighted

14 All the .... in this school are between five and nine years old.
   A pupils   B people   C students   D candidates

15 Hannah is .... to go back home at the end of her course.
   A wanting   B wishing   C desiring   D longing

16 Susanna did well in the test because she had .... so thoroughly for it.
   A trained   B prepared   C studied   D worked

17 I just can't eat chillis. They're too .... for me.
   A hot   B spicy   C tasty   D burning

18 Ronald was .... by the police for stealing a tennis racket.
   A charged   B summoned   C arrested   D punished

19 They said the accident was Andrea's ....
   A fault   B blame   C responsibility   D action

20 The .... of the disagreement was a misunderstanding between the boss
   and the accounts department.
   A reason   B cause   C explanation   D outbreak

21 Robert parked where it was forbidden and had to pay a ....
   A penalty   B subscription   C fine   D fee

22 I didn't enjoy the film and Henry didn't ....
   A either   B neither   C as well   D also

23 Shirley's the best tennis player .... has been selected from that club.
   A who   B that   C which   D whose

24 The student behaved .... he was really annoyed.
   A like   B though   C so   D as if

25 The ice will melt if the temperature ....
   A rises   B will rise   C has risen   D will have risen

Use of English

1 *Fill each of the numbered blanks in the following passage. Use only* **one** *word in each space.*

When the writer Daniel Defoe published *The Life and Adventures of Robinson Crusoe* in 1719, he based his tale on the story of what .... (1) happened to Alexander Selkirk, ... (2) man who had left his home to .... (3) his living as a sailor and had spent five years alone on the island of Juan Fernandez in the Pacific.

In the book, ... (4) ship on which the hero .... (5) travelling sank in a violent storm. Robinson Crusoe .... (6) to escape from the ship and .... (7) a desert island. There, alone, because everyone .... (8) on the ship had drowned, he had to learn to survive. Defoe describes in vivid detail .... (9) Crusoe went .... (10) coming to terms with his environment. .... (11) the tools he had saved from the wrecked ship, Crusoe built .... (12) a house and also a boat in .... (13) he could sail around the island, though could not escape from it. .... (14) were some goats on the island, and Crusoe domesticated them, ... (15) that he had milk and meat to live on.

Robinson Crusoe had .... (16) spent twenty-five years on the island .... (17) it was visited by a group of cannibals. He was shocked by what they did and he saved one of their prisoners from .... (18) killed. This man, who Crusoe .... (19) Friday, became his companion and helper. With Friday by his side Crusoe was able to forget the loneliness he had suffered. Finally, some three years .... (20), an English ship came to the island and Crusoe and Friday were rescued.

2   *Finish each of the following sentences in such a way that it means exactly the same as the sentence printed before it.*

    EXAMPLE: I haven't enjoyed myself so much for ages.

    ANSWER: *It's ages since I enjoyed myself so much.*

a) Jennifer doesn't have as much luggage to carry as the others.

    Jennifer has ....

b) Would you like to come to the concert with me?

    Are you interested ....

c) Despite the bad weather, the mountaineers set off for the summit.

    Although ....

d) I'd rather not go out this evening.

    I'd prefer not ....

e) John is not old enough to join the Boy Scouts.

    John is too ....

f) How long have they been building that house?

    When ....

g) If you want my opinion, it would be a good idea to stop eating so many sweets.

    If I ....

h) 'I don't think you told me the truth about Sylvia,' said Julia to Alexander.

    Julia accused Alexander ....

i) People say that he is an excellent saxophone-player.

    He ....

j) It's Constantine's fault that the tickets were lost.

    Constantine ....

3 *Complete the following sentences with a phrase made from* **take**. *Write one word in each blank space.*

    EXAMPLE: He *took off* his shoes.

a) These boxes are .... too much space in the office.

b) Mr Leech will .... the accounts department when Mr Burgess retires.

c) The lecturer gave us so many facts and figures we just couldn't .... them all ....

d) It was the first time he had tried cross-country ski-ing, but he .... it immediately.

e) You'll have to .... the legs .... the table before moving it down the stairs.

4 *The word in capitals at the end of each of the following sentences can be used to form a word that fits suitably in the blank space. Fill each blank in this way.*

    EXAMPLE: He was *famous* as a singer of romantic songs.   FAME

a) There is a .... of fresh strawberries at this time of year.

                                                                              SCARCE

b) The manager reluctantly accepted the .... of closing the factory down.   NECESSARY

c) Mr Callaghan experienced a feeling of great .... as he left his office for the last time.   SAD

d) During his lifetime there was no .... of his vital contribution to scientific knowledge.   RECOGNISE

e) I think the .... of this word is incorrect.   SPELL

5 *Marianne is talking to Thomas about his holiday. Complete the dialogue.*

MARIANNE   Thomas, Shirley tells me you've just got back from the States. Did you (1) ....?

THOMAS   Yes, it was absolutely great. It's the best holiday I've ever had.

MARIANNE   Where (2) ....?

THOMAS   Well, I flew to New York, spent three days there, and then got on a Greyhound bus and spent two weeks touring the eastern states.

MARIANNE   What's (3) ....?

THOMAS   Well, it's good really. Most well-off Americans like to travel by car, but lots of other people use the bus. And it's quite comfortable, and air-conditioned. And you can travel quite long distances, overnight if you want to.

MARIANNE   Did (4) ....?

THOMAS   Just once. I wouldn't want to do it too often. It's too tiring. But giving up one good night's sleep meant I got an extra day in Boston.

MARIANNE   What (5) ....?

THOMAS   I'd have to say that it was Lake Michigan in Chicago. It was like a sea. It just knocked me out. And the buildings were so impressive too.

MARIANNE   Was (6) ....?

THOMAS   Not really. Food was cheap and so was travelling by bus. And there are a lot of modest hotels that are quite cheap if two of you share a room. I'd recommend a trip like that to everyone.

Test 7

Reading Comprehension, Section A

Choose the word or phrase (A, B, C, or D) which best completes each sentence.

1 The Council demolished the .... and built modern houses on the same site.
A suburbs   B outskirts   C blocks   D slums

2 The water was so .... we could see right to the bottom of the lake.
A clear   B limpid   C clean   D lucid

3 The cinema is on your right and the Town Hall is directly ....
A opposite   B over   C in front of   D facing

4 When Dobbs Broughton first met Antoinette Demolines he was surprised to find that she was .... more beautiful than he had expected.
A fairly   B so   C rather   D very

5 A .... of £10,000 was offered for information leading to the arrest of the bank robbers.
A reward   B prize   C award   D remuneration

6 The immigration officer .... my passport.
A controlled   B evaluated   C analysed   D checked

7 When Martin decided to sell his car he placed a(n) .... in the local newspaper.
A announcement   B advertisement   C message   D note

8 This oil refinery has increased its .... by 12% this year.
A produce   B products   C producing   D production

9 The house has been .... since the owner died last year.
A unpopulated   B uninhabited   C free   D unoccupied

10 How long we stay here depends .... the weather.
A of   B for   C about   D on

11 .... much you have to pay, you must buy the diamond and bring it here.
A Whatever   B However   C Whoever   D Whichever

12　There are three spelling .... in this composition.
　　A faults　　B wrongs　　C mishaps　　D mistakes

13　Please remember that George will be .... holiday next week.
　　A in　　B going　　C on　　D having

14　It's getting very late, so I think I'll go .... now.
　　A home　　B to home　　C for home　　D at home

15　Mr Arnold .... his hotel bill just after breakfast.
　　A paid for　　B paid off　　C paid　　D paid in

16　Chess was a .... at which Richard excelled.
　　A play　　B sport　　C match　　D game

17　After driving for three hours we stopped .... lunch at a restaurant.
　　A having　　B to have　　C have　　D for having

18　Four .... three equals twelve.
　　A by　　B times　　C multiplied　　D across

19　Eric was really interested .... Ancient Egypt.
　　A in　　B for　　C by　　D to

20　The plans for the invasion are not .... complete.
　　A still　　B already　　C yet　　D now

21　Martin had never driven .... a fast car before.
　　A so　　B so far　　C such as　　D such

22　I suggest .... an hour earlier this Friday.
　　A finishing　　B finish　　C to finish　　D the finish

23　You will need a .... more eggs to make that cake.
　　A little　　B few　　C deal　　D least

24　After forgetting his keys three days running, Adrian began to worry about how
　　.................... he was getting.
　　A absent-minded　　B thoughtless　　C unthinking　　D distracted

25　You must remove your shoes before you .... this building.
　　A enter　　B will enter　　C entering　　D entered

Use of English

1 *Fill each of the numbered blanks in the following passage. Use only* **one** *word in each space.*

In 1928 Amelia Earhart became famous as the first woman to fly from America to Europe. On .... (1) occasion she was a passenger but in 1932 .... (2) the age of thirty-five, she became the first woman to fly solo .... (3) the Atlantic. Amelia Earhart was a university graduate, could speak five languages and was married .... (4) a wealthy publisher, but she was also an expert pilot who was determined to fly long-distance routes .... (5) had not been attempted before.

In 1935 she began a round-the-world flight, starting in California and heading west, but she crashed .... (6) take-off in Honolulu and had to .... (7) up the attempt. However, in 1937 she decided to .... (8) again, this .... (9) in the opposite direction. A month after .... (10) California, she was in New Guinea, preparing for the flight to Howland Island, a tiny Pacific island .... (11) no aircraft had ever landed. The distance .... (12) these two points was over 4,000 kilometres, further than anyone had .... (13) non-stop before. Amelia and her navigator, Fred Noonan, knew that if they .... (14) to find Howland Island they would run out .... (15) fuel somewhere over the Pacific.

Ships positioned near the island picked .... (16) radio signals from Amelia's aircraft, but it never landed and, after a time, ... (17) became clear that it .... (18) no longer be in the air. For two weeks, there was a thorough search of the area, but nothing was ever .... (19) and to this day .... (20) knows exactly what happened to Amelia Earhart and Fred Noonan.

2 *Finish each of the following sentences in such a way that it means exactly the same as the sentence printed before it.*

    EXAMPLE: I haven't enjoyed myself so much for ages.

    ANSWER: It's ages *since I enjoyed myself so much.*

a) I have never visited this museum before.

    This is ....

b) Frank continued to phone Emily even though she had told him she never wanted to hear from him again.

    Frank kept ....

c) Michael took a packed lunch on his walk because he thought he might be hungry.

    Michael took a packed lunch in case ....

d) This letter was written by Thomas Hardy.

    Thomas Hardy ....

e) The police have advised car owners to fit an alarm in their cars.

    Car owners have received ....

f) Mr Mitchell's company is always busier in August than in any other month.

    August is ....

g) 'Which path did the bandits take?' asked the Sheriff.

    The Sheriff asked ....

h) What a pity it rained on Helen's wedding day.

    I wish it ....

i) It was such a surprise for his mother to see Tom that she burst into tears.

    Tom's mother was so ....

j) In Wales we saw Edward II's birthplace.

    In Wales we saw the castle ....

3 *Complete each of the following sentences with* **one** *appropriate word connected with the subject of* **crime**.

   EXAMPLE: The *murderer* buried his victims in waste ground.

   a) If you .... the law, you must expect to be punished.

   b) Anyone found guilty of committing a crime will be given a ....
       by the judge.

   c) Many householders now install alarms to deter .... from enter-
       ing their houses.

   d) Car .... is increasing throughout the country and drivers are
       advised to protect their vehicles.

   e) George was .... for attacking another football supporter.

4 *The word in capitals at the end of each of the following sentences can be used to form
   a word that fits suitably in the blank space. Fill each blank in this way.*

   EXAMPLE: He was *famous* as a singer of romantic songs.   FAME

   a) If you wish to visit military camps, you will require .... from
       Army personnel.   AUTHORITY

   b) Joan couldn't swim and when she fell into the pool all she could do was to
       splash ....   HELP

   c) I'm afraid there was some delay in finding the information for you as the
       records have not yet been ....   COMPUTER

   d) Jim's action in giving all his Christmas presents to charity was regarded by
       his parents as ....   PRAISE

   e) You can't have access to these files without the boss's ....

                                                                    PERMIT

5 *Make all the changes and additions necessary to produce, from the following sets of words and phrases, sentences which together make a complete letter. Note carefully from the example what kind of alterations need to be made. Write each sentence in the space provided.*

> EXAMPLE: I be very surprised/receive/letter/you yesterday.
>
> ANSWER: I was very surprised to receive a letter from you yesterday.

3 Addison Road
Surbiton
Surrey KT1 3JL

The Manager
Claims Department
Universal Insurance plc
12 Priory Court
London EC2   14 August 19– –

Dear Sir or Madam

Policy Ref. No. BA/15/JK/1581

I write/give/full details/theft/camera/cassette-player/car.

a) ....

I drive/wife/two friends/Box Hill/Surrey/Sunday 12 August.

b) ....

We left/car/car-park/bottom/hill/after take out/things we need/picnic.

c) ....

Before leave/car we hide/camera/cassette-player/front seats/lock/doors.

d) ....

About two hours later we return/picnic/find/window smash/both items/steal.

e) ....

Apart/window/there be no damage/car.

f) ....

The two items/steal be almost new/I enclose/receipts/shop I buy/.

g) ....

I insure/company/more/ten years/I be confident you be able/offer/adequate compensation/loss.

h) ....

Yours faithfully

George Knightley

Test 8

Reading Comprehension, Section A

Choose the word or phrase (A, B, C, or D) which best completes each sentence.

1 I don't know how much it would cost to buy that painting, it's absolutely
....
A valuable   B invaluable   C worthwhile   D priceless

2 The doctor .... Harriet that she should have an operation to correct the
problem in her arm.
A advised   B explained   C suggested   D insisted

3 Jane .... spending the afternoon at the swimming pool.
A urged   B encouraged   C suggested   D persuaded

4 They .... Stephen for the accident.
A blamed   B faulted   C accused   D charged

5 The garage intended to .... £300 to repair the car.
A cost   B charge   C bill   D debit

6 All members of .... should report to the Personnel Department for information about the new rates of pay.
A workforce   B employees   C staff   D company

7 Could you .... me how the machine works?
A show   B indicate   C explain   D draw

8 That college has a high ....
A name   B renown   C opinion   D reputation

9 Mr Francis, the boss, has a high .... of himself.
A opinion   B status   C view   D belief

10 It had been Sarah's lifelong .... to visit India.
A fantasy   B need   C desire   D ambition

11 Jane was bitterly .... not to get the job.
A deceived   B disappointed   C depressed   D disturbed

12 The author spent all day long staring at a .... sheet of paper.
    A white   B empty   C clear   D blank

13 The murderer shot his victim in cold ....
    A blood   B anger   C revenge   D fury

14 To cook spaghetti you should immerse it in .... water.
    A bubbling   B hot   C warm   D boiling

15 The fruit is kept in a .... in the dining room.
    A bowl   B plate   C container   D jar

16 What .... of car would you buy if you could?
    A make   B variety   C mark   D brand

17 The prisoner escaped from the high-security prison by .... the guards.
    A corrupting   B enticing   C bribing   D charming

18 Harry .... his father in his love of gardening.
    A takes after   B looks like   C follows after   D stands by

19 Many students save money on air travel by buying .... tickets.
    A take-off   B stand-by   C pick-up   D lift-off

20 The alarm was .... by accident when the builders were repairing the house.
    A turned on   B rung up   C sounded off   D set off

21 If you don't know what the word means, ... in the dictionary.
    A look it up   B search it out   C find it out   D chase it up

22 .... often Mary goes jogging, she never seems to lose weight.
    A Whenever   B How   C As   D However

23 Film stars .... as Frank Sinatra and Robert Redford have been ready to
    support the candidate they want to be President of the USA.
    A so   B like   C being   D such

24 This is simply the best ice-cream I have .... tasted.
    A ever   B still   C never   D so far

25 Shirley looked through the rack of dresses and .... out three to try on.
    A threw   B stood   C turned   D picked

Use of English

1 *Fill each of the numbered blanks in the following passage. Use only **one** word in each space.*

Romeo and Juliet are the two young lovers famous throughout the world because of the play that Shakespeare wrote about their love story. The story takes .... (1) in Verona, Italy. Romeo is a member of the Montague family .... (2) Juliet is a member of the Capulets. For many years there has been bitter disagreement .... (3) the two families.

When Romeo and Juliet meet, they immediately .... (4) in love with .... (5) other. They want to get .... (6), but because of the bad feeling that exists between the two families, they realise that their wedding .... (7) have to take place in secret. A priest, Friar Lawrence, ... (8) the ceremony. .... (9) the day of the wedding, there is a fight in the street and Romeo kills Tybalt, a relative of Juliet's. .... (10) a punishment, he is ordered to go away to live in another city.

Juliet's father, ignorant of Juliet's marriage to Romeo, wants her to marry someone .... (11). As part of a plan to .... (12) this, Juliet, with the help of Friar Lawrence, takes some medicine that makes it seem as .... (13) she is dead. The plan is .... (14) Romeo will rescue her. But .... (15) Romeo hears that Juliet has really died. He comes back to Verona to see Juliet for the .... (16) time, takes poison and dies. Juliet wakes up and finds him .... (17). She kills .... (18) with a knife.

The parents of .... (19) young people are .... (20) shocked by the tragedy that they decide to end their quarrel.

2 *Finish each of the following sentences in such a way that it means exactly the same as the sentence printed before it.*

     EXAMPLE: I haven't enjoyed myself so much for ages.

     ANSWER: It's ages *since I enjoyed myself so much.*

a)   This is the last time I will speak to you.

     I ....

b)   Given the choice between tea and coffee, I'd drink tea.

     I'd rather ....

c)   The train was delayed because of the snow, so Thomas was late for the meeting.

     If the train ....

d)   It is essential that Dr Barker is called immediately.

     Dr Barker ....

e)   All the competitors know that they will be disqualified if they are found taking drugs.

     Every ....

f)   Mr Corleone is the most highly paid director.

     None of the other directors ....

g)   'Saddle your horses, men!' said the captain.

     The captain ordered ....

h)   I'm not happy with the idea of Chris going on a 48-hour camping trip in the mountains.

     I'd rather ....

i)   I don't think it's possible you saw Alice in the street yesterday because she went to work abroad last month.

     You can't ....

j)   I spent three hours trying to find the source of that quotation.

     It ....

3   *Complete each of the following sentences with words which refer to a **place** where things can be bought. Write one word in each blank space.*

   EXAMPLE: If you want stamps, you must go to the *post office.*

   a)   Tom went to the .... in the High Street because he wanted to make arrangements for the family holiday in Spain.

   b)   Many consumers find it more convenient to shop at large .... where there is a wide range of goods, competitive prices and good parking facilities, than to buy things from their small local grocery store.

   c)   Although we can't get fresh fish in our town, we have four .... selling fresh meat.

   d)   I need some petrol. Can you tell me where the nearest .... is?

   e)   Joan always likes to do her shopping in ...., where you can find everything from clothes to household goods and from toys to food.

4   *The word in capitals at the end of each of the following sentences can be used to form a word that fits suitably in the blank space. Fill each blank in this way.*

   EXAMPLE: He was *famous* as a singer of romantic songs.   FAME

   a)   Tony would be more popular with his teachers if he behaved less
   ....   POLITE

   b)   The people whose houses are to be demolished when the new road is built will be .... outside the city.   HOUSE

   c)   I think my .... was the happiest time of my life.   CHILD

   d)   Mmm. This pudding is very ....   TASTE

   e)   It was always Ronald's ambition to become a .... advisor.
          FINANCE

5 *Make all the changes and additions necessary to produce, from the following sets of words and phrases, sentences which together make a complete letter. Note carefully from the example what kind of alterations need to be made. Write each sentence in the space provided.*

EXAMPLE: I be very surprised/receive/letter/you yesterday.

ANSWER: *I was very surprised to receive a letter from you yesterday.*

Room 512
William Barnes Hall
University of Exeter
Exeter EX2 1AP

The Manager
Royal Hotel
The Esplanade
Plymouth PM4 8QT   30 April 19– –

Dear Mr Vine

I write/enquire/possibility/job/waitress/Royal Hotel.

a) ....

A friend/mine, Maria Peters, work/you last summer.

b) ....

She tell me what she do/I like/know/you need waitresses this year.

c) ....

I be nineteen years old/present I study French/University/Exeter.

d) ....

The university vacation begin/June 22/I must return/Exeter/October 5.

e) ....

Therefore, I be available/work/months/July, August/September.

f) ....

I look forward/receive details/rate/pay, hours/working conditions.

g) ....

Can you confirm/there be living accommodation/waitresses/hotel?

h) ....

I enclose/stamped, addressed envelope/reply.

i) ....

Yours sincerely

Bathsheba Everdene

Test 9

Reading Comprehension, Section A

Choose the word or phrase (A, B, C, or D) which best completes each sentence.

1 The room measured four metres .... five metres.
  A cross   B times   C multiplied   D by

2 When he telephoned from the airport Mr Jones was told that the hotel was ....
  A complete   B full   C occupied   D crowded

3 Achilles and his men walked silently past the .... guards.
  A sleeping   B asleep   C slept   D sleeper

4 Mrs Miller is .... her first baby at the end of March.
  A expecting   B waiting   C hoping   D having

5 .... a lovely present! Thank you very much!
  A How   B What   C So   D That

6 He re-arranged the pillows and sheets so that it looked .... someone was in the bed.
  A as well as   B as a matter of fact   C as if   D so as

7 He is .... intelligent to be taken in by such a trick.
  A very   B enough   C too   D quite

8 What do you .... me to do about my lost luggage?
  A suggest   B advise   C encourage   D tell

9 .... his illness, he managed to finish the project on time.
  A Although   B In spite   C However   D Despite

10 Peter's prompt telephone call to the Gas Board .... a disaster from occurring.
  A prevented   B averted   C avoided   D diverted

11 Deborah works .... a speech-writer for the Prime Minister.
  A as   B as if   C like   D being

12 During my time as chairman of this company I have found Lord Gladstone's advice absolutely ....
A priceless   B valuable   C precious   D invaluable

13 If you have a moment to ...., could you look through today's post?
A waste   B spare   C spend   D lose

14 At the beginning of the class, the teacher called out the names on the ....
A list   B register   C form   D class

15 At the end of a day's walking in the Scottish Highlands we looked for a .... where we could put up our tent.
A camping   B camping-place   C camp-site   D camper

16 Jennifer was very .... to Bob and Rachel for all the help they had given her.
A grateful   B thankful   C pleased   D welcoming

17 All the people at the meeting expressed their .... of the new arrangements.
A agreement   B satisfaction   C approval   D pleasure

18 When spring came the snow and ice began to ....
A dissolve   B evaporate   C liquefy   D melt

19 Mr Brown is paid more than £50,000 .... year.
A the   B all   C plus   D a

20 He .... to sign the statement the police put in front of him.
A denied   B disagreed   C refused   D negated

21 Scientists estimate that the satellite will .... Jupiter in three years' time
A reach   B arrive   C take   D get

22 If Sally works really hard she should be able to make .... the time she lost through absence.
A out   B up   C in   D back

23 The Channel Tunnel is the first physical .... between the United Kingdom and France.
A join   B link   C tie   D attachment

24 The actor was offered the .... of Hamlet in a new production of Shakespeare's famous play.
A part   B paper   C script   D character

25 A small problem has .... in connection with the renewal of the visa.
A risen   B raised   C risen up   D arisen

Use of English

1 *Fill each of the numbered blanks in the following passage. Use only **one** word in each space.*

In 1749, after living in Ecuador for thirteen years, Jean Godin decided to return to France with his Peruvian wife, Isabella. However, ... (1) his wife was pregnant and unable to travel, Jean set off .... (2) her, intending to send a ship .... (3) her later. He sailed down the Amazon to Cayenne in French Guyana. Unfortunately, because of bureaucratic delays, it was not until 1765 that Jean .... (4) in arranging for a ship to collect his wife, and not until 1769 that Isabella received news that a Portuguese ship .... (5) waiting for her at a port along the river Amazon. In .... (6) to reach this ship, Isabella had to travel several hundred miles by canoe.

She set off with her two brothers, a nephew, four servants and three Frenchmen who .... (7) the party at .... (8) last moment. During the journey, they were abandoned by their guides and all their canoes were destroyed in accidents. In .... (9) of suffering from hunger, illness and exhaustion, they .... (10) to build .... (11) canoe and two of the Frenchmen .... (12) ahead to get help, while the rest of the party stayed behind. After four weeks, help .... (13) not come, ... (14) Isabella and her companions built a raft, but it capsized and all their food and belongings were lost. They started to travel overland, but all .... (15) Isabella died .... (16) hunger and exhaustion.

After walking for twenty days, Isabella reached a village .... (17) she obtained a canoe and guides .... (18) took her to the Portuguese ship .... (19) had waited five years for her. In 1770, she arrived .... (20) Cayenne and was re-united with her husband, twenty-one years after she had last seen him.

2 *Finish each of the following sentences in such a way that it means exactly the same as the sentence printed before it.*

      EXAMPLE: I haven't enjoyed myself so much for ages.

      ANSWER: It's ages *since I enjoyed myself so much.*

a)   This is the first time I have been to a casino.

     I ....

b)   Alison travelled to China because she wanted to study medicine there.

     Alison travelled to China so ....

c)   Oliver doesn't expect to get the job.

     Oliver would be surprised ....

d)   No-one has signed this certificate.

     This..

e)   John and Mary don't realise how dangerous it is to walk in the mountains without proper equipment.

     Neither ....

f)   I didn't think there would be such a lot of furniture in the house.

     There is ....

g)   'We didn't expect so many people to come,' said the chairman.

     The chairman said ....

h)   The rally driver regrets not training hard enough in ice and snow.

     The rally driver wishes ....

i)   Too many eggs are bad for you.

     You..

j)   It was only April but the sea was so warm we went swimming.

     The sea was warm ....

3 *Complete the following sentences with a phrase made from* **put**. *Write one word in each blank space.*

EXAMPLE: It's getting dark. Please *put* the light *on*.

a)   I don't mind washing up but I just hate .... the dishes ....

b)   The Chairman had flu so it was decided to .... the meeting .... for a week.

c)   Despite the use of men from two fire brigades, it took over twelve hours to .... the fire in the chemical factory ....

d)   'Look, Sheila, I'll be in Edinburgh next week. Do you think you could possibly .... me .... for a few nights?'

e)   Andy and Charlotte decided to go and live in a sunny climate. They just couldn't .... English weather any more.

4 *Complete each of the following sentences with one word which refers to part of a* **house**.

EXAMPLE: Juliet stood on the *balcony* and looked down at Romeo.

a)   When he opened the front door and stepped into the ...., he saw that the living-room was through the first door on his right.

b)   As Peter reached up to paint the .... drops of paint dripped on to his face and arm.

c)   During the storm a number of .... were blown off the roof.

d)   It was impossible to light a fire because the previous owner of the house had blocked up the ....

e)   The reason there are cracks in the wall is that the .... of the house are beginning to subside.

5 *A customer brings a cassette-player into a shop. Complete the dialogue.*

SHOP ASSISTANT Good morning, sir.

CUSTOMER Good morning. I was given this mini cassette-player as a birthday present, but I can't get it to work.

SHOP ASSISTANT (1) What ....?

CUSTOMER When I press the buttons absolutely nothing happens.

SHOP ASSISTANT (2) Could ....?

CUSTOMER I don't think so. I tried it with four different cassettes and it was just the same.

SHOP ASSISTANT (3) Did ....?

CUSTOMER Oh, yes. It only works on batteries anyway. There are two in this compartment here. Have a look!

SHOP ASSISTANT (4) I think you ....

CUSTOMER Oh really! How silly of me! Well, I'm not very technically-minded.

SHOP ASSISTANT (5) I'm sure ....

CUSTOMER Oh, good. Can I just try it before I leave the shop?

SHOP ASSISTANT Certainly. (6) Let's ....

CUSTOMER That sounds perfect. Thank you very much.

Test 10

Reading Comprehension, Section A

Choose the word or phrase (A, B, C, or D) which best completes each sentence.

1 After the meeting a large .... of keys was found on one of the seats.
   A bunch   B bundle   C pile   D load

2 Instead of driving through the town it would be quicker to use the ....
   A subway   B underpass   C flyover   D bypass

3 John always buys fresh fish at a .... in the market.
   A kiosk   B stand   C stall   D cabin

4 The pop concert was .... when the local council refused permission for the use of the site.
   A cancelled   B stopped   C prevented   D forbidden

5 Sally wanted to get a job in finance so she took a .... in Business Studies.
   A career   B training   C formation   D degree

6 We can offer lots of holidays in Spain. See if there are any you like in this ....
   A catalogue   B brochure   C directory   D prospectus

7 This is the most boring TV programme I've ever seen. Can't we see what's on the other .... ?
   A band   B station   C frequency   D channel

8 The champion athlete had his medal taken away when he was discovered to have been ....
   A cheating   B tricking   C deceiving   D defrauding

9 Even .... Anna was upset about the accident, she still managed to carry on with her work.
   A so   B as   C when   D though

10 Sharon's the girl .... boyfriend has been selected for the next Olympics.
   A whose   B of whom   C who's   D which

11 John travelled twenty miles to get to the hospital to visit his sister, Susan, ... was thoughtful of him.
   A that   B which   C who   D what

12 These are tablets for a sore throat. You must .... them slowly.
    A swallow   B suck   C chew   D bite

13 My aunt had decided to buy the expensive china vase but then she discovered
    a .... down the side.
    A crack   B damage   C mark   D chip

14 The chimney was damaged in the storm so Alison decided to put in a ....
    to the insurance company.
    A demand   B request   C form   D claim

15 It was so late, we thought the postman wouldn't come, but he finally ....
    at 11.30.
    A turned up   B came up   C ran up   D drove up

16 The mechanic carefully .... the car out of the garage.
    A turned   B directed   C manipulated   D backed

17 I was .... in the middle of my telephone conversation with the Director.
    A put through   B hung up   C rung off   D cut off

18 Jane .... on her journey to Tibet well-equipped with all the necessary
    supplies.
    A set out   B got off   C went out   D started up

19 The alarm .... and the police realised that there was an intruder in the
    empty house.
    A went off   B set off   C rang off   D turned off

20 Applicants for the job must have a .... driving licence.
    A clear   B pure   C untouched   D clean

21 Jonathan and his mother have always been very ....
    A close   B near   C attached   D intimate

22 Mrs Brown's purse was very heavy because it was full of small ....
    A pieces   B money   C change   D currency

23 When Mr Frederick retired after twenty years in the Accounts Department, his
    .... gave him a gold watch.
    A employees   B team-mates   C officers   D colleagues

24 The rally driver lost .... of the car and it skidded off the road.
    A command   B power   C concentration   D control

25 When young children watch TV it's difficult for them to distinguish between
    the programmes and the ....
    A commercials   B propaganda   C publicity   D advertisers

Use of English

1   *Fill each of the numbered blanks in the following passage. Use only **one** word in each space.*

In most major cities in the world, violence is accepted as a feature of daily life. Stories of robbery and personal attack are common and .... (1) crime figures are taken for granted. But a recent phenomenon is causing concern in Britain, ... (2) of rural violence. In small country towns, usually considered to be peaceful and trouble-free, outbreaks of violence .... (3) becoming more frequent. This violence is .... (4) various kinds: sometimes it's Saturday night drunkenness, with young people having .... (5) much to drink and then fighting with .... (6) another or attacking property; at other times there are attacks .... (7) minority groups; occasionally there is shooting by people who have got hold of .... (8). The police in rural areas are now having to deal with situations with .... (9) they were formerly unfamiliar.

Why .... (10) these young people turn to violence? .... (11) parents put the blame on TV but another explanation may be boredom. Young people who live far from big metropolitan centres .... (12) an age where they want to break out of the small world where they .... (13) up. They need to be .... (14) to get about on .... (15) own, to travel beyond their villages not only for leisure .... (16) also for access to work and further education. If they can't afford transport, there is .... (17) major problem. Many country teenagers are trapped by distance. There are now fewer buses than sixty years ago, and they don't .... (18) late in the evening. .... (19) is little to do in the villages themselves, especially in the winter.

They'll grow out of it, their parents say, and of course they .... (20). But it isn't much fun, having little money and nothing to do in a beautiful place that for them is a social desert.

2 *Finish each of the following sentences in such a way that it means exactly the same as the sentence printed before it.*

EXAMPLE: I haven't enjoyed myself so much for ages.

ANSWER: It's ages *since I enjoyed myself so much.*

a) How long has Mr Inglis been in hospital?

When ....

b) I don't think it's a good idea to go to bed late the night before the exam.

If I ....

c) They didn't want to be late for the meeting so they left in plenty of time.

So as ....

d) All the pupils in the school want to go on the skiing holiday in the Alps.

Every ....

e) Nobody can deny that he is the best artist of the twentieth century.

It ....

f) Tony hasn't got enough money to buy the computer he really wants.

The computer ....

g) 'Put your tents between the river and the forest,' said the instructor to the scouts.

The instructor old ....

h) Alastair's sorry that he can't come to the concert tonight.

Alastair wishes ....

i) Being rude to the policeman wasn't the right thing to do.

You shouldn't ....

j) May 5 is their wedding day.

They ....

3　*Complete each of the following sentences with one word which refers to* **physical discomfort**.

　　EXAMPLE:　People who stay in the sun for too long suffer from *sunburn*.

　a)　If you've got a head- .... you should take some aspirins.

　b)　Peter's got a .... throat and has to keep sucking pastilles and throat sweets.

　c)　The .... in Sarah's leg was so bad that she couldn't sleep.

　d)　Maria had an infected tooth and her whole face was ....

　e)　Jonathan .... his back doing too much digging in the garden.

4　*The word in capitals at the end of each of the following sentences can be used to form a word that fits suitably in the blank space. Fill each blank in this way.*

　　EXAMPLE:　He was *famous* as a singer of romantic songs.　　FAME

　a)　The language .... in the school felt that Tom should see a speech therapist for help with his difficulties.　　ADVISE

　b)　Sally finally realised that her husband was a .... as a businessman when the second company he had set up collapsed.　　FAIL

　c)　John was leading the race, and everyone thought he would win but .... he tripped and fell thirty yards from the winning post.　　FORTUNE

　d)　When I was ill, I couldn't have managed without Frank. His help was ....　　VALUE

　e)　If you want a job with a good salary you will find .... better paid than your present post.　　ADMINISTER

5　*Make all the changes and additions necessary to produce, from the following sets of words and phrases, sentences which together make a complete letter. Note carefully from the example what kind of alterations need to be made.*

　　EXAMPLE:　I be very surprised/receive/letter/you yesterday.

　　ANSWER:　I was very surprised to receive a letter from you yesterday.

17 Athelney Road
Melchester
Wessex MC3 4AD

The Curator
Museum of Science and Technology
Brunel Road
Melchester
Wessex MC8 2JE   2 June 19– –

Dear Sir or Madam

I visit/museum/my two nephews, aged seven/ten, / Tuesday 30 May.

a) ....

I be very surprised/I have/pay/total/£6/gain admission/museum.

b) ....

I be sure/when I last visit/museum two years ago admission be completely free.

c) ....

Perhaps/museum be obliged/charge/cover/costs.

d) ....

However, it not improve/service/public/any way.

e) ....

I notice/museum cafe be still not open/hour after/museum itself open.

f) ....

When I take/nephews/cafe we find/coffee be nearly cold/cakes be not fresh.

g) ....

Moreover, many/exhibits be not/working order/several parts/museum be closed.

h) ....

I also observe/museum shop/only sell guide-books/English,/many foreign tourists come/Melchester.

i) ....

In return/admission fee I think/public be entitled/higher standard/service.

j) ....

Yours faithfully

Michael Faraday

Key

For each test there is a total number of 100 marks. The marks are divided in the following way:

Reading Comprehension, Section A
One mark for each correct answer (total = 25 marks).

Use of English
Question 1: one mark for each correct answer. Answers must be spelt correctly. No mark will be given if you give more than one answer. (total = 20 marks)

Question 2: marks are indicated in the key. A mark is given for each group of words in *italics*. Groups are separated by a space. (total = 20 marks)

Question 3: one mark for each correct answer. Correct spelling is essential. (total = 5 marks)

Question 4: one mark for each correct answer. All parts of the answer must be correct, including spelling and tense. (total = 5 marks)
Question 5: in the telegram letter subtract half a mark for each error, from a total of 25 marks. In the dialogue completion exercises subtract one mark for each error, from a total of 25 marks.

If you score more than 55 marks on a whole test you are probably ready to take the examination.

Test 1

Reading Comprehension, Section A

1	A
2	C
3	C
4	D
5	A
6	A
7	D
8	B
9	C
10	A
11	A
12	D
13	C
14	D
15	B
16	C
17	D
18	A
19	A
20	C
21	A
22	D
23	B
24	D
25	C

Use of English

1
1	the/ his
2	chose/ bought/selected
3	by
4	a
5	nearby
6	and
7	least
8	worthless/ stolen/forged/ counterfeit
9	leaving
10	suddenly
11	that
12	decided
13	than
14	did
15	was
16	even

17 him
18 going
19 for
20 which

2 A mark is given for each group of words in *italics*. Groups are separated by a space. For example , in *Question a* one mark is given for *visited Peru* and another mark for *for*.

  a) I haven't *visited Peru for* five years. (*2 marks*)

  b) You'd better *buy* a dictionary *if you want* to learn a foreign language. (*2 marks*)

  c) Who *does this pen belong   to?* (*2 marks*)

  d) Rosalind is such *a   hard worker* that she is sure to get on in her job. (*2 marks*)

  e) This machine *records* electrical activity in the brain. (*1 mark*)

  f) If you *don't eat up* your vegetables, *you won't get* any pudding. (*2 marks*)

  g) Despite *being / the fact that he was* over seventy, *Alfred continued* to cycle to work every day. (*2 marks*)

  h) Bernard accused *Sebastian   of   stealing/having stolen* the video-recorder. (*3 marks*)

  i) I have *never tasted   a   better* apple pie (than this one). (*3 marks*)

  j) I'd rather *you didn't invite* Mary to stay for the weekend. (*1 mark*)

3 a) bring about
  b) brought it back
  c) bring the subject up
  d) bring him round
  e) brought out

4 a) operator
  b) extension
  c) engaged
  d) directory
  e) dial

5 a) A friend of mine who attended your school from 1986 to 1987 has recommended it to me.

  b) I want to spend a year in England improving/to improve my English before going / I go to university.

  c) I have already studied English for six years at school.

  d) I would / should like to attend a course/courses in general English for/during the first two terms and then study Business English.

  e) I am interested in taking exams while I am at the school.
  I would be interested in taking exams while I am/was at the school.

  f) Could you tell me what exams I can/could enrol for and if I will/would have to pay to enter them?

  g) Finally, could you send me a prospectus giving/with full details of how much everything will/would cost?

  h) I hope to hear from you soon.

Test 2

Reading Comprehension, Section A

1 A
2 D

3 B
4 B
5 D
6 B
7 C
8 A
9 B
10 D
11 C
12 A
13 C
14 A
15 B
16 A
17 D
18 D
19 A
20 B
21 C
22 D
23 A
24 B
25 C

Use of English

1 1 living/existing
   2 was
   3 together
   4 get
   5 expecting
   6 a
   7 away
   8 birth
   9 bringing
   10 her
   11 willing/ready
   12 who
   13 managed
   14 has
   15 for
   16 at
   17 They
   18 both
   19 fact
   20 with

2 a) The winter in England is not *warm enough for* gardeners to leave geraniums outside. (*2 marks*)

b) Peter's grandfather has *lived / been living* in England *for* fifty years. (*2 marks*)

c) The fireman was *able to rescue* the child from the burning house. (*2 marks*)

d) Stephen prefers *windsurfing to sailing*. (*3 marks*)

e) Unless Peter *is invited*, Mary *will not / won't come* to the party. (*2 marks*)

f) It's time we *left the party if* we are to catch the last bus. (*2 marks*)

g) Michael apologised *to Geraldine for losing her* book. (*3 marks*) Michael apologised *for losing Geraldine's* book.

h) You have *to check* the patient's temperature every hour. (*1 mark*

i) I haven't got *enough money to buy* that suit. (*2 marks*)

j) Although *he didn't speak* a word of French, Jeremy decided to make his home in Paris. (*1 mark*)

3 a) get it across
   b) get on with
   c) getting round/over
   d) get at
   e) got away with

4 a) slippery
   b) pronunciation
   c) membership
   d) signature
   e) products

5 a) It was lovely to hear from you on Monday.

b) Martin and I were/are delighted to learn about/of your forthcoming wedding.

c) Of course we would absolutely love to be there on the big day, but unfortunately it is just impossible.

d) In July Martin is attending a conference in San Francisco in California on/ about new developments in electronics.

e) He has arranged for me to go with him and almost all the arrangements have now been made.

f) We are/shall be staying in the States after the conference to go/ and going on a tour of five more states.

g) I am very sorry that this means we shall not be at your wedding, but you know that you have our very best wishes.

h) We have already posted your present and we hope you and Karl will like it.

Test 3

Reading Comprehension, Section A

1 A
2 C
3 B
4 B
5 A
6 A
7 B
8 C
9 D
10 D

11 C
12 D
13 D
14 A
15 C
16 B
17 C
18 D
19 C
20 A
21 C
22 D
23 C
24 D
25 B

Use of English

1
1 on
2 although
3 was
4 for
5 nearest
6 which/that
7 breaking/broken
8 according
9 During
10 by
11 if/when
12 reached
13 they
14 another/an
15 there
16 and
17 to
18 for
19 of
20 all

2 a) Whose *bicycle is this?* (*1 mark*)
Whose *is this bicycle*?

b) Would you like *to go* for a walk in the park? (*1 mark*)

c) I haven't *seen* a play by Christopher Marlowe *for* more than ten years. (*2 marks*)

d) It was *such cold weather* that

people only went out if they had to. (*1 mark*)

e) 'I'm *sorry I'm late*', *said Alison.* (*3 marks*)

f) In spite *of having* only one arm, *Frederick became* famous as a mountaineer. (*3 marks*)

g) No-one *in the class has read* more books *than* Margaret. (*3 marks*)

h) If Henry *went*/*had been* to the dentist for regular check-ups he *wouldn't have* toothache. (*2 marks*)

i) These shoes haven't *been mended yet.* (*3 marks*)

j) I wish *I had a new dress* to wear to the party. (*1 mark*)

3 a) make for
b) make out
c) made the story up
d) make up for
e) make out

4 a) faulty
b) fitness
c) removal
d) weight
e) valuable

5 1 How *can I get there?*
2 Isn't *there any other way?*
  Isn't *there a cheaper way?*
3 How *much does it cost?*
  How *much is that?*
  How *much is it?*
4 How *often do the trains run?*
5 How long *does the journey take?*
  How long *does it take to get there?*
6 Are *these the only ways to get there?*
7 So which *is the cheapest way?*

Test 4

Reading Comprehension, Section A

1	A
2	C
3	B
4	D
5	C
6	A
7	C
8	B
9	A
10	A
11	D
12	A
13	B
14	A
15	D
16	C
17	C
18	A
19	B
20	A
21	D
22	A
23	C
24	A
25	D

Use of English

1	1	in
	2	on
	3	as/ because/ since
	4	with/carrying
	5	her
	6	gave/offered
	7	asked
	8	to
	9	there
	10	when
	11	Suddenly/Then
	12	get
	13	had
	14	a
	15	decided

16 home
17 first
18 still
19 felt
20 and

2 a) When *did you start/begin* reading *Don Quixote*? *(1 mark)*

b) By *working extremely hard* Peter managed to get promoted to the job of Office Manager. *(1 mark)*

c) If it *hadn't   been raining / rained,   we could have seen* Mont Blanc. *(3 marks)*

d) The shelf is too high *for me   to reach.* *(2 marks)*

e) There *is   no milk (left)*. *(2 marks)*
There *isn't   any milk (left)*.

f) That's the house Charles Dickens lived *in from* 1840 to 1850. *(1 mark)*

g) Tom *must have   cleared* everything up. *(2 marks)*
Tom *must have been   the one who cleared* everything up.

h) The ship *was   broken* in two *by* an enormous wave. *(3 marks)*

i) The other students have *further   to travel   than* Christabel. *(3 marks)*

j) Although *he lacks   experience*, I think he is the best man for the job. *(2 marks)*

3 a) turned up
b) turn back
c) turning into
d) turned down
e) turned out

4 a) application
b) labels
c) register/list

d) statement
e) invitation

5 a) Well, Stephen and I have finally moved into our new flat in Oxford and we really love it.

b) The flat is quite near the centre but we do not seem to get any noise.

c) We have got a sitting-room, two bedrooms, a kitchen and a bathroom, in fact everything we need for a perfect home.

d) We would like you to come and see us as soon as you possibly can.

e) As you can see, we have even got a spare room for you to stay in.
As you can see, we have even got a spare room which you can stay in.

f) We were wondering if next weekend would be convenient for you as it would suit us perfectly.

g) We will be at home every evening this week.

h) So just give us a ring if it is.

Test 5

Reading Comprehension, Section A

1   C
2   A
3   A
4   D
5   B
6   A
7   C
8   D
9   A
10 D
11 B

12   B
13   C
14   C
15   D
16   A
17   B
18   C
19   A
20   D
21   D
22   B
23   B
24   D
25   D

Use of English

1 1   ruled
2   on
3   who
4   However
5   the
6   wife/queen
7   to
8   but
9   later
10   during
11   as
12   until/till
13   all
14   from
15   led
16   in
17   by
18   themselves
19   a
20   than

2 a) The bag was light *enough for* Mary's three-year old son *to carry*. (*3 marks*)

b) In spite *of   being injured/having been injured* in the crash he managed to walk twenty kilometres to get help. (*2 marks*)

c) Robert's boss gave him *such*

good advice that Robert would be foolish to ignore it. (*2 marks*)

d) October 23 is *Barbara's   twenty-fifth   birthday*. (*3 marks*)

e) Thomas asked *why   he had to* fill in so many forms. (*2 marks*)

f) I got *less* information *than* I wanted. (*2 marks*).

g) The aeroplane *was flown* for the first time *by* Squadron-Leader Bigglesworth. (*2 marks*)

h) I wonder if you'd mind *opening* the window. (*1 mark*)

i) Unless *I hear* from you, I'll assume you can't come to the meeting. (*1 mark*)

j) My grandfather has *not driven   for* five years. (*2 marks*)

3 a) fallen out
b) fallen through
c) fall behind
d) fell for
e) fell in with

4 a) success
b) security
c) qualifications
d) proud
e) strength

5 a) I am writing to you to say how dissatisfied I was with the holiday from which I have just returned.

b) The holiday in Marbella was booked with/through your company in January.

c) I understood that my husband, my/our two children and I would fly/would be flying from Manchester at twelve noon and that we would spend/would be spending fourteen days at Hotel Esplendido in Marbella.

d) We chose Hotel Esplendido because it had a private swimming pool, was near the beach and offered a baby-sitting service for the children.

e) Our flight from Manchester was delayed for twenty-four hours and we had to spend the time in the Departure Lounge.

f) When we finally got to Marbella, the/your representative told us we had been moved to Hotel Blanco which was a forty-five minute walk from the beach.

g) We are not satisfied with the way we have been treated and want to know what action you intend to take.

h) We expect/are expecting a refund for at least part of the cost of the trip.

i) We look forward to hearing your response.

Test 6

Reading Comprehension, Section A

1	A
2	C
3	D
4	A
5	C
6	B
7	A
8	D
9	D
10	A
11	B
12	A
13	B

14	A
15	D
16	B
17	A
18	C
19	A
20	B
21	C
22	A
23	B
24	D
25	A

Use of English

1
1	had
2	a
3	earn
4	the
5	was
6	managed
7	reach
8	else
9	how
10	about
11	Using/With
12	himself
13	which
14	There
15	so
16	already
17	when
18	being
19	called/named
20	later

2
a) Jennifer has *less luggage* to carry *than* the others. (*2 marks*)

b) Are you interested *in coming* to the concert with me? (*2 marks*)

c) Although *the weather was bad*, the mountaineers set off for the summit. (*2 marks*)

d) I'd prefer not *to go out* these evening. (*1 mark*)

e) John is too *young   to join* the Boy Scouts.   (*2 marks*)

f) When *did they start* building that house?   (*1 mark*)

g) If I *were you,   I would stop eating* so many sweets.   (*2 marks*)

h) Julia accused Alexander *of   not telling/having told   her* the truth about Sylvia.   (*3 marks*)

i) He *is said   to be* an excellent saxophone-player.   (*2 marks*)

j) Constantine *is to blame   for   losing* the tickets.   (*3 marks*)

3 a) taking up
    b) take over
    c) take them all in
    d) took to
    e) take the legs off

4 a) scarcity
    b) necessity
    c) sadness
    d) recognition
    e) spelling

5 1 Did you *have a nice/good time?*
       Did you *enjoy yourself/it?*
    2 Where *did you go?*
    3 What's *it like travelling by Greyhound/on a Greyhound bus?*
    4 Did *you ever travel overnight?*
    5 What *was the best/most impressive thing you saw?*
    6 Was *it expensive/an expensive trip?*

Test 7

Reading Comprehension, Section A

1 D
2 A

3	A
4	C
5	A
6	D
7	B
8	D
9	D
10	D
11	B
12	D
13	C
14	A
15	C
16	D
17	B
18	B
19	A
20	C
21	D
22	A
23	B
24	A
25	A

Use of English

1
1	that
2	at
3	across
4	to
5	which/that
6	on
7	give
8	try
9	time
10	leaving
11	where
12	between
13	flown
14	failed
15	of
16	up
17	it
18	could
19	found
20	no-one/nobody

2 a) This is *the first time I have visited* this museum. (*3 marks*)

b) Frank kept (*on*) *phoning* Emily even though she had told him she never wanted to hear from him again. (*1 mark*)

c) Michael took a packed lunch in case *he was* hungry. (*2 marks*)

d) Thomas Hardy *wrote this letter*. (*2 marks*)

e) Car owners have received *advice from the police* to fit an alarm in their cars. (*2 marks*)

f) August is always *the busiest* month for Mr Mitchell's company. (*2 marks*)

g) The Sheriff asked *which path the bandits took/had taken*. (*2 marks*)

h) I wish it *hadn't rained* on Helen's wedding day. (*2 marks*)

i) Tom's mother was so *surprised to see him* that she burst into tears. (*2 marks*)

j) In Wales we saw the castle *where/in which Edward II was born*. (*2 marks*).

3 a) break
b) sentence
c) burglars
d) theft
e) arrested

4 a) authorisation
b) helplessly
c) computerised/computerized
d) praiseworthy
e) permission

5 a) I am writing to give you full details of the theft of my/a camera and cassette-player from my car.

b) I drove (with) my wife and two friends to Box Hill in Surrey on Sunday, 12 August.

c) We left our/the car in the car-park at the bottom of the hill after taking out the things we needed for the/our picnic.

d) Before leaving the/our car we hid the camera and cassette-player under the front seats and locked (all) the doors.

e) About two hours later we returned from our picnic to find/and found (that) a window had been smashed and both items (had been) stolen.

f) Apart from the window there was no damage to the car.

g) The two items which/that were stolen were almost new and I enclose the receipts from the shop where/from which I bought them. *or* . . . (which/that) I bought them from.

h) I have been insured with your company for more than ten years and I am confident you will be able to offer me adequate compensation for my/this loss.

Test 8

Reading Comprehension, Section A

1   D
2   A
3   C
4   A
5   B
6   C
7   A
8   D
9   A
10 D
11 B

12 D
13 A
14 D
15 A
16 A
17 C
18 A
19 B
20 D
21 A
22 D
23 D
24 A
25 D

Use of English

1
1 place
2 while/whereas/and/but
3 between
4 fall
5 each
6 married
7 will
8 performs
9 On
10 As
11 else
12 avoid
13 if/though
14 that
15 instead
16 last
17 dead
18 herself
19 the
20 so

2 a) I *will not speak to you* again. (*2 marks*)

b) I'd rather *drink tea than coffee.* (*2 marks*)

c) If the train *hadn't been delayed John wouldn't have been late* for the meeting. (*2 marks*)

d) Dr Barker *must be called* immediately. (*2 marks*)

e) Every *competitor knows (that) he/ she will be disqualified if he/she is found* taking drugs. (*3 marks*)

f) None of the other directors *is paid as much/so highly as* Mr. Corleone. (*2 marks*)

g) The captain ordered *the/his men to saddle their horses.* (*3 marks*)

h) I'd rather *John didn't go* on a 48-hour camping trip in the mountains. (*2 marks*)

i) You can't *have seen* Alice in the street yesterday because she went to work abroad last month. (*1 mark*)

j) It *took me* three hours *to find* the source of that quotation. (*2 marks*)

3 a) travel agent('s)/agency
b) supermarkets
c) butchers(')
d) garage/petrol station/filling station
e) department stores

4 a) impolitely
b) rehoused
c) childhood
d) tasty
e) financial

5 a) I am writing to enquire about the possibility of a job as a waitress at the Royal Hotel.

b) A friend of mine, Maria Peters, worked for you last summer.

c) She (has) told me what she did and I would like to know if you need waitresses this year.

d) I am nineteen years old and at present I am studying French at the University of Exeter.

e) The university vacation begins on June 22 and/but I must return to Exeter on/by October 5.

f) Therefore, I am/will be available for work during the months of July, August and September.

g) I look forward to receiving details of the rate of pay, hours and working conditions.

h) Can you confirm that there is living accommodation for waitresses at the hotel?

i) I enclose a stamped, addressed envelope for your reply.

Test 9

Reading Comprehension, Section A

1	D
2	B
3	A
4	A
5	B
6	C
7	C
8	B
9	D
10	A
11	A
12	D
13	B
14	A
15	C
16	A
17	C
18	D
19	D
20	C
21	A
22	B
23	B
24	A
25	D

Use of English

1
1	as, since, because
2	without
3	for
4	succeeded
5	was
6	order
7	joined
8	the
9	spite
10	managed
11	another/a
12	went
13	had
14	so
15	except/but
16	of/from
17	where
18	who
19	which/that
20	in

2 a) I *have never been to* a casino *before*. (*2 marks*)

b) Alison travelled to China so *that she could study* medicine there. (*1 mark*)
Alison travelled to China so *as to study* medicine there.

c) Oliver would be surprised *if he got the job*. (*2 marks*)

d) This *certificate has not been signed*. (*2 marks*)

e) Neither *John nor Mary realises* how dangerous it is to walk in the mountains without proper equipment. (*2 marks*)

f) There is *much more furniture* in the house *than I had expected*. (*2 marks*)

g) The chairman said (*that*) *they had not expected* so many people to come. (*2 marks*)

h) The rally driver wishes *(that) he had trained harder* in ice and snow.   (*2 marks*)

i) You *shouldn't eat too many eggs*.   (*2 marks*)

j) The sea was *warm enough for us   to go swimming* although/ even though it was only April. (*3 marks*)

3 a) putting the dishes away
 b) put the meeting off
 c) put the fire in the chemical factory out
 d) put me up
 e) put up with

4 a) hall
 b) ceiling
 c) tiles/slates
 d) fireplace/chimney
 e) foundations

5 1 What's *wrong with it?*
  What's *the problem?*
 2 Could *there be something wrong with the cassette (you are using)?*
  Could *it be the cassette (you are using)?*
 3 Did *you put (new) batteries in?*
 4 I think you *(may) have put the batteries in the wrong way round.*
 5 I'm sure *it will work/be all right now.*
 6 Let's try it (out).
  Let's give it a try.

Test 10

Reading Comprehension, Section A

 1 A
 2 D
 3 C
 4 A

 5 D
 6 B
 7 D
 8 A
 9 D
 10 A
 11 B
 12 B
 13 A
 14 D
 15 A
 16 D
 17 D
 18 A
 19 A
 20 D
 21 A
 22 C
 23 D
 24 D
 25 A

Use of English

1 1 rising/high
 2 that
 3 are
 4 of
 5 too
 6 one
 7 on
 8 guns
 9 which
 10 do/should
 11 Their/Many/Some
 12 reach
 13 grew
 14 able
 15 their
 16 but
 17 a
 18 run
 19 There
 20 will

2 a) When *did Mr Inglis go to hospital?*   (*1 mark*)

 b) If *I were you, I wouldn't go to*

bed late the night before the exam.
(*2 marks*)

c) So as *not to be late for the
meeting,   they left in plenty of
time.*   (*2 marks*)

d) Every *pupil in the school   wants*
to go on the skiing holiday in
the Alps.   (*2 marks*)

e) It *cannot   be denied* that he is the
best artist of the twentieth
century.   (*2 marks*)

f) The computer *Tony really wants
is   too expensive   for him to buy.*
(*3 marks*)

g) The instructor told *the scouts   to
put their tents* between the river
and the forest.   (*2 marks*)

h) Alastair wishes *he could come* to
the concert tonight.   (*2 marks*)

i) You shouldn't *have been rude* to
the policeman.   (*2 marks*)

j) They *will get married   on May
5.*   (*2 marks*)
They *are getting married   on May
5.*
They *are going to get married   on
May 5.*
They *get married   on May 5.*

3 a) ache
   b) sore
   c) pain
   d) swollen
   e) hurt/strained

4 a) advisor
   b) failure
   c) unfortunately
   d) invaluable
   e) administration

5 a) I visited your museum with my
      two nephews, aged seven and ten,
      on Tuesday 30 May.

   b) I was very surprised that I had to
      pay a total of £6 to gain admission
      to the museum.

   c) I am sure that when I last visited
      the/your museum two years ago
      admission was completely free.

   d) Perhaps the/your museum is
      obliged to charge (in order) to
      cover its costs.

   e) However, it has not improved its
      service to the public in any way.

   f) I noticed (that) the museum cafe
      was still not open an hour after
      the museum itself had opened.

   g) When I took my nephews to the
      cafe we found (that) the coffee was
      nearly cold and the cakes were not
      fresh.

   h) Moreover, many of the exhibits
      were not in working order and
      several parts of the museum were/
      had been closed.

   i) I also observed (that) the museum
      shop only sells/sold guide-books
      in   English,   although/(even)
      though many foreign tourists
      come to Melchester.

   j) In return for the admission fee I
      think the public is entitled to a
      higher standard of service.